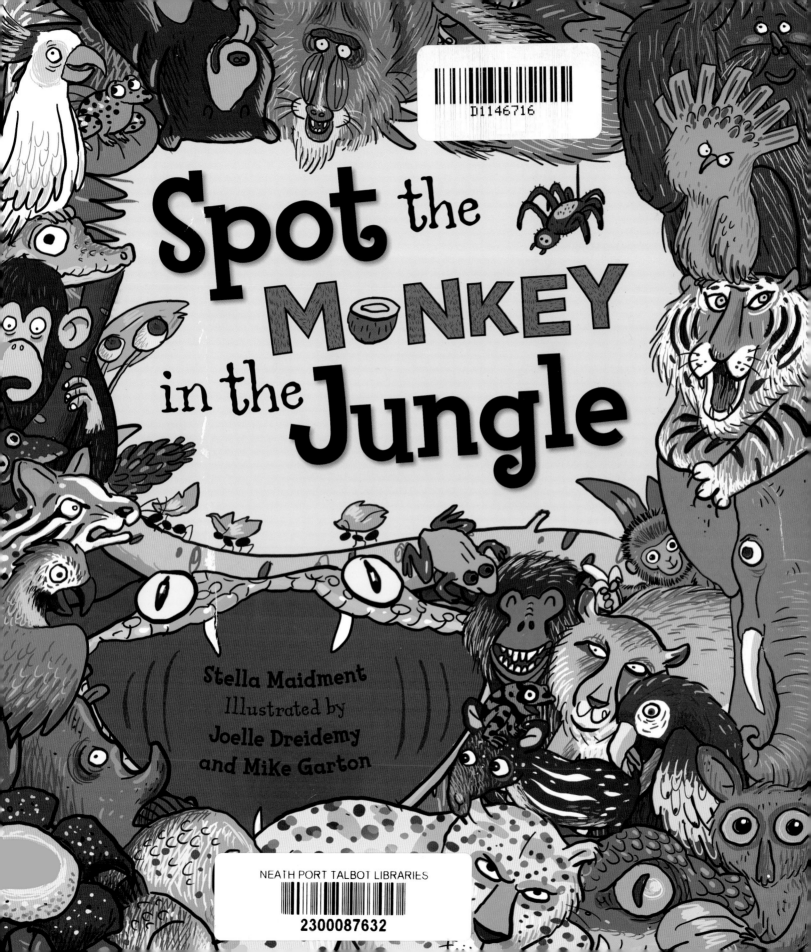

Spot the MONKEY in the Jungle

Stella Maidment

Illustrated by
Joelle Dreidemy
and Mike Garton

Thunderstorm

Night-time

Monkeys

Flowers

Jungle floor

This baby monkey is hiding inside the book. Can you find him in every scene?

Crocodiles often sleep with their mouths open. Sometimes little birds fly in and pick the meat off their teeth!

One of the biggest flowers in the world is called Rafflesia. It's red with spots, and it smells horrible!

In the treetops you'll see
the laziest animal in the jungle.
The three-toed sloth can sleep
for up to 20 hours a day!

Can you spot these things?

toucan   blue butterfly   iguana   snail   green parrot

Can you see the golden lion tamarin? It has yellow fur around its face like a lion's mane.

Poison dart frogs are beautiful but very dangerous. Some types have enough poison to kill ten people.

It rains a lot in the jungle but the clever orang-utans use leaves to make a roof over their nest.

Thousands of
different sorts of fruit
grow in the jungle.

Can you spot these things?

watermelon

rhinoceros beetle

lime

star fruit

pink butterfly

Baby tapirs have special spots and stripes to help them blend in and keep them safe while they are young.

At night some creatures sleep, while others come out to hunt for food.

More to spot

Go back and find these scenes in the book!

Did you find me?

Did you Know?

Gorillas laugh when they are tickled!

Explorers in the African jungle never wear dark blue or black because these colours attract dangerous tsetse flies.

About 30 million types of insect live in the Amazon jungle, with probably lots more still to be discovered!

When a baby elephant is born, its aunts, sisters and female cousins all help its mother to look after it.

Every tiger has a stripy coat but each one is slightly different. No two tigers have the same markings.

More jungle fun!

Make a jungle poster

Make a 3D jungle background by collecting leaves and sticking them on a piece of paper. Now draw and colour your favourite jungle creatures. You could copy some from this book. Cut them out and stick them on to your poster.

Snake puppet

Use an old long sock. Put your fingers into the toe section and your thumb in the heel to make the snake's mouth. Glue on a red paper tongue and some circles of cardboard or foil for eyes.

Hide and seek

Choose a cuddly toy that you can hide around your home for a friend or family member to spot, just like the monkey in the book! You could hide other objects and make a list of things to find.

Animal guessing game

Ask an adult to write the names of ten different jungle animals on ten slips of paper. The first player chooses one and then has to act like the animal, but without speaking or making any noise! Everyone else tries to guess what it is.

Designer: Krina Patel
Editor: Tasha Percy
Editorial Director: Victoria Garrard
Art Director: Laura Roberts-Jensen

Copyright © QED Publishing 2014

First published in the UK in 2014 by
QED Publishing
A Quarto Group company
The Old Brewery,
6 Blundell Street,
London, N7 9BH

www.qed-publishing.co.uk

A catalogue record for this book is available from the British Library.

ISBN 978 1 78171 654 0

Printed in China